CW00421122

Published by Red Squirrel Publishing
Suite 235, 77 Beak Street,
London, W1F 9DB, United Kingdom

www.redsquirrelbooks.com

First edition published in 2008

ISBN 978-0-9552-1597-1

10 9 8 7 6 5 4 3 2 1

Edited by Alastair Smith
Proofreading by Frances King and Richard Walshe
Cover design by Emma Barnes
Designed by Cox Design Limited, Witney, Oxon

Printed and bound in Great Britain by J. H. Haynes & Co. Ltd., Sparkford

CONTENTS

FOREWORD

BY DAVID EDGAR

I became interested in citizenship tests when I was looking for a way of writing about Britishness. I'd written a play about the northern English riots of 2001 for the National Theatre, which had been rehearsed and performed against the background of the 7/7 bombing attacks on the London underground and growing fears that Britain was "sleepwalking into segregation". The following January, I was at a Fabian Society conference, at which Gordon Brown sought to revitalise the idea of Britishness in the contemporary world. Clearly, an idea whose time seemed to have gone had come back with a vengeance.

It didn't take me long to come round to citizenship tests as a way of exploring what Britishness was, is and could be. I already knew about the American test, in which would-be citizens were quizzed on the composition of the US Senate, the Declaration of Independence, and the Bill of Rights. I'd vaguely heard that some German states were wanting to ask Muslims about their views on homosexuality and the holocaust. I remembered that Home Secretary David Blunkett had introduced a Britishness test which had been attacked from several directions, but I had no idea of its contents.

In fact – unlike the tests of most countries – the actual questions are a closely guarded secret. As I discovered, there are only four official samples on the government's Life in the UK website, designed to demonstrate the different forms of question. The subjects of these specimen questions are the Prime Minister's official residence, the voting age, how to get a National Insurance number and where you can use Scottish banknotes.

As the questions are based on five chapters of one book, the Life in the UK handbook, first published in 2004 and substantially revised in 2007, it is easy to work out the questions that the tests must (and do) contain. This is the third of three editions of sample tests produced by Red Squirrel Publishing. Obviously, they were and are intended to help aspirant citizens to pass the citizenship test. But, along with the handbook, they paint a fascinating picture of what the British think Britishness is, or, more importantly, what they think it ought to be.

That a supposedly objective, factual test can reveal what a country thinks of itself is shown clearly by comparing the British test with others. As stated, the American test largely deals with the country's history, constitution and current governmental structures. The first big section of the Canadian handbook A Look at Canada is about taking care of the environment (the message is: good Canadians separate their trash). The German state of Baden-Wuttenberg did indeed propose asking people what they thought about homosexuality, forced marriages and wife-beating. While Hesse wanted to ask would-be immigrants to list three German mountain ranges and to identify the central motif of a famous landscape painting of a Baltic island; a test clearly designed to be impossible to pass.

The British test, by contrast, has little about geography,

culture (or sport) and excludes history entirely. So, strictly, prospective citizens don't need to read the first chapter of the Life in the UK handbook, which tells our island story. But anyone who is interested in how we view ourselves should not only read it, but compare the versions in the two editions of the book. The first, written by Professor Bernard Crick (political commentator and biographer) was elegant, erudite and witty. The second version, revised by civil servants, wasn't.

So, the first edition starts: "To understand a country well and the character of its inhabitants, some history is needed. We are influenced more than we imagine by images of the past, true or false, historical or legendary". In the second edition, this sentence has been edited down to: "To understand a country it is important to know something about its history". The revised version edition has much more about immigration, much less about the virtues of empire. The new edition adds an entire section on the 18th-century enlightenment, a period whose principles are close to the heart of the current government.

The post-history section of the book (on which people are tested) continues the same strategy. "Everyone has the right to religious freedom" becomes the more circumspect "people are usually very tolerant towards the faiths of others". A section on engagement before marriage is taken out, a section on community cohesion (including Red Nose Day) put in. More significantly, in view of the changing climate of the times, is that "The police are there to be helpful" has been changed to "All good citizens are expected to help the police".

The reason why history was dropped from the test was

partly to evade controversy: British historians are seriously divided about the character and even course of the national story. It was also felt important to concentrate on things about Britain that would be helpful to potential immigrants.

The result is a test that contains much useful, practical information. But in order to avoid controversy, the test gives a very limited and sometimes skewed view of the life it's trying to describe. Life in the UK tells you how to get your neighbour evicted, but doesn't suggest that you might ask her to water your roses. Most striking is a list of "key terms and vocabulary" that the assiduous student needs to understand in Chapter Two of the second edition (A Changing Society), which includes hazards, molestation, misuse, abuse, addictive substances, binge-drinking, heroin, cocaine, ecstasy, amphetamines, burglary, mugging, racism and terrorism. Welcome to our world.

All right, I'm being selective. But it's legitimate to ask why so much of the handbook presents the UK as a thicket of rules and a minefield of risk. Why, even in the bits that aren't tested on, are its authors so nervous about presenting the UK as a place with a personality, part of which is about being open and welcoming?

Inevitably, countries want newcomers to see them in their best light. The Americans are proud of their history and constitution, the Canadians of their wilderness, the Germans of their artists. Our nervousness about these subjects leads to a suspicion that what we value in our country is under threat from the very people who want to join us. The Life in the UK history section makes clear that Britain was a land of immigration long before it was – in any constitutional sense – Britain, and that it has remained so ever since. The rest of the handbook demonstrates (if you dig for it) that we have a long tradition of civil liberties, which have been fought for by our ever-changing people and defended against attack.

When I was researching my citizenship play (Testing the Echo) I attended classes at which prospective citizens learn the English they need to meet the language requirements of citizenship. I asked them what they admired about their new home, and their answer was precisely those values – decency, fair play, democracy, liberty – which critics regard as either too vague or too universal to be meaningful. The paradox is that it is precisely those values which – it sometimes seems – are under threat because the newcomers are here.

David Edgar's play Testing the Echo *was toured by the Out of Joint theatre company from January to May 2008.*

INTRODUCTION

In November 2005, the British Government introduced the Life in the United Kingdom Test. Its introduction sparked immediate public and media interest as it was labelled a test of "Britishness". The obvious question raised was, "What is Britishness?"

Of course, the test was never intended to be a test of "Britishness". Its intention is to assess an applicant's knowledge of life in the United Kingdom and grasp of English (or Welsh or Scottish Gaelic). But the knowledge of the country which they have to demonstrate is not general knowledge. It is drawn from a government-issued handbook, which they have to study in detail. To pass they must correctly answer at least 18 out of 24 multiple-choice questions.

All questions are drawn from the handbook. The handbook covers a range of topics on life in this country, in particular, demographics, customs, traditions, government, employment and aspects of everyday life. Although the official questions set by the government are not available for public view and are a closely guarded secret, the questions in this book have been used by hundreds of thousands of people to help them pass the test.

For many people, the test is seen as a pub quiz of random information selected by the government. Some people also argue that many British-born citizens would fail the test. Whatever your view of the test, this book provides an informative, if not quirky, insight into the route to a new British life that most native Brits would take for granted.

Anyone lucky enough to be born in Britain will never have to worry about taking the citizenship test – but if you did, would you pass it?

CHAPTER 1: A CHANGING SOCIETY

The questions in this chapter deal with recent changes in British society. Primarily, the chapter is about the way British society has evolved since the end of the Second World War. Society has changed markedly in that time, both culturally and in terms of the ethnic make-up of the population. You need to know how different groups (particularly ethnic) have contributed to society, and the role that they have played in the changes that have occurred in society, since the War. Some of the most obvious changes have been the result of mass immigration. Immigration involved groups from many parts of the world and occurred in varying ways. You will need to know how and why this happened. What motivated people to come here and why did Britain invite them to come?

Another area of huge social change in Britain has been at family level. Women have gained more rights and responsibilities, and, as that has occurred, family dynamics have had to change as well. Women have become more active in politics, education and the workplace. This has meant changes in the way that women participate in their more traditional family roles, especially in terms of childcare. Britain is also a very different place to live for young people than it was not long ago. Children and young people face a whole new set of challenges today as they progress through the education system and become young adults.

Most British people should find the questions from this chapter familiar, but to be successful you will need to know some specific information, particularly relating to the arrival of major immigrant groups.

1 Why was there a fall in the number of people migrating to the UK from the West Indies, India, Pakistan and Bangladesh in the late 1960s?

A New laws were introduced restricting immigration to Britain

B It was becoming more difficult for immigrants to find employment in the UK

C These countries were experiencing labour shortages

D A weak British currency made immigration less appealing

2 Why did Protestant Huguenots from France come to Britain?

A To invade and seize land

B To escape religious persecution

C To seek refuge from war

D To escape famine

3 What percentage of the workforce are women?

A 40%

B 45%

C 51%

D 65%

4 On average, boys leave school with better qualifications than girls. Is this statement true or false?

A   True

B   False

5 Which of these statements is correct?

A   In the 1960s and 1970s Parliament passed laws giving women the right to equal pay

B   In the 1960s and 1970s Parliament passed laws allowing employers to discriminate against women because of their gender

6 When were women given voting rights at the same age as men?

A   1928

B   1945

C   1918

D   1840

7 When did the First World War end?

A   1914

B   1945

C   1918

D   1925

8 When were women over 30 given the right to vote?

A   1918

B   1945

C   1901

D   1840

9 Who were Suffragettes?
  A Campaigners for greater rights for women
  B Refugee care workers
  C Representatives of people seeking asylum
  D Nurses that cared for the elderly

10 When did married women gain the right to retain ownership of their own money and property?
  A 1792
  B 1810
  C 1752
  D 1882

11 What year did women in the UK gain the right to divorce their husband?
  A 1945
  B 1810
  C 1901
  D 1857

12 Which of these statements is correct?
  A Women have always had the same rights as men
  B In 19th-century Britain, women had fewer rights than men

13 There are more men studying at university than women. Is this statement true or false?
  A True
  B False

14 During the 1980s, the largest immigrant groups to the UK came from which countries?

A China, Japan and South Korea

B Russia, Poland, Belarus and Ukraine

C India, Pakistan, Sri Lanka and Bangladesh

D United States, Australia, South Africa and New Zealand

15 Very few people believe that women in Britain should stay at home and not go out to paid work. Is this statement true or false?

A True

B False

16 From which two locations did Britain admit refugees during the late 1960s and early 1970s?

A Uganda

B Turkey

C South East Asia

D Ethiopia

17 Why did the UK set up recruitment centres in the West Indies during the 1950s?

A To recruit workers to drive buses

B To recruit workers to build railways

C To recruit workers to build canals

D To recruit workers for textile factories

18 Why did the UK encourage immigration in the 1950s?

A To resolve a shortage of labour in the UK

B Because of an agreement with other Commonwealth countries

C To offer safety to people escaping persecution

D To meet an EU directive on immigration

19 During the 1950s, textile and engineering firms from the UK sent recruitment agents to which two countries? Select two countries from below

A Poland

B Pakistan

C South Africa

D India

20 How long was Britain at war during the Second World War?

A 4 years

B 8 years

C 2 years

D 6 years

21 **The government encouraged immigrant workers from where to help British reconstruction after the Second World War?**
A   Australia and other parts of Oceania
B   America and other parts of North America
C   Ireland, other parts of Europe and the West Indies
D   India, Pakistan and Bangladesh

22 **When was the Second World War?**
A   1840–1846
B   1901–1918
C   1939–1945
D   1919–1925

23 **Why did large numbers of Jewish people come to Britain during 1880–1910?**
A   To escape famine
B   To escape racist attacks
C   To invade and seize land
D   To work in textile factories

24 **Name three countries that Jewish people migrated from (and into the UK) to escape persecution during 1880–1910**
A   China, Japan, Korea
B   Israel, Egypt, Jordan
C   USA, Canada, Mexico
D   Poland, Ukraine, Belarus

25 **Why did Irish migrants come to Britain during the mid 1840s?**
- A To escape famine
- B To seek refuge from war
- C To escape religious persecution
- D To invade and seize land

26 **In Scotland, when do most young people take SQA examinations?**
- A 17 years old
- B 15 years old
- C 16 years old
- D 18 years old

27 **Which of these statements is correct?**
- A It is legal to possess cannabis in the privacy of your own home
- B It is illegal to possess cannabis anywhere

28 **Which of these statements is correct?**
- A It is illegal to be drunk anywhere
- B It is illegal to be drunk in public

29 **What is the minimum age for buying tobacco?**
- A 20 years old
- B 14 years old
- C 18 years old
- D 21 years old

30 **How many children are estimated to be working in the United Kingdom?**

A   Eight million

B   Five million

C   Two million

D   One million

31 **What are the most common jobs that children in Britain do? Select two answers from below**

A   Deliver newspapers

B   Work in hospitals or pharmacies

C   Work in supermarkets or newsagents

D   Work in kitchens

32 **What is a "gap year"?**

A   A measurement used by the government to assess literacy

B   A period of time taken by a young person to work or travel before starting university

C   The first year a young person spends at university

D   A year of study that has to be repeated

33 **What proportion of young people go on to higher education after school?**

A   All young people move on to higher education

B   One in four

C   One in three

D   One in two

34 **There are more women than men in Britain's population. Is this statement true or false?**

A False

B True

35 **In England, when do most young people take GCSE examinations?**

A 18 years old

B 16 years old

C 15 years old

D 17 years old

36 **What proportion of young people who became first-time voters in the 2001 general election actually used their vote?**

A One in five

B One in six

C One in three

D One in two

37 **In Scotland, when do most young people take Higher/Advanced Higher Grades?**

A 15 and 16 years old

B 10 and 11 years old

C 17 and 18 years old

D 13 and 14 years old

38 **At what ages do teachers formally assess children's progress in Wales?**

A 6 and 10

B 8 and 12

C 5 and 10

D 7 and 11

39 **At what age do school children take their first national test in Wales?**

A 14

B 11

C 9

D 7

40 **Which of these statements is correct?**

A It is compulsory for children aged between 5 and 16 to receive full-time education

B Children aged over 14 do not have to receive full-time education

41 **What percentage of children in the UK live with both birth parents?**

A 25%

B 40%

C 65%

D 80%

42 **What percentage of children live in lone-parent families?**

A 10%

B 25%

C 40%

D 55%

43 **What percentage of children live within a stepfamily?**

A 10%

B 25%

C 40%

D 55%

44 **How often do most children in the UK receive their pocket money?**

A Every day

B Every week

C Every month

D Only on their birthday

45 **How many young people (up to the age of 19) are there in the UK?**

A 5 million

B 10 million

C 15 million

D 20 million

46 **What is the difference in the average hourly pay rate for men and women?**

A The average hourly pay rate is 5% lower for women

B The average hourly pay rate is 10% lower for women

C The average hourly pay rate is 20% lower for women

D No difference – the average hourly pay rate for women is the same as men

47 **Despite existing laws, women still do not always have the same access to promotion and better paid jobs as men. Is this statement true or false?**

 A False

 B True

48 **What proportion of women with children (of school age) are in paid work?**

 A Half

 B Two thirds

 C One quarter

 D Three quarters

49 **Which of these statements is correct?**

 A Some young people work to pay for their university fees and expenses

 B University education is free to anyone who wishes to study

CHAPTER 2:
UK TODAY – A PROFILE

This chapter is in essence a basic summary of the main demographic and cultural characteristics of British society as it is today. Questions from this chapter will test your knowledge of the people who live in this country now and the things that make them who they are, such as ethnicity, religions, traditions and customs. In other words, how they live their lives on a daily basis. A particular focus is on the four nations of the United Kingdom and their associated cultural traditions. The range of religious practices, customs and traditions that exist in modern Britain is also important.

The customs and traditions that the questions from this chapter focus on should be familiar to most British people. However, the detailed facts and figures about the country that must be known to answer the questions may be another matter. A perusal of summary data from a recent census would be a huge advantage.

50 **Welsh is no longer taught in schools in Wales. Is this statement true or false?**
A False
B True

51 **When is the national day for England?**
A 23 April
B 30 November
C 1 March
D 17 March

52 **What is the distance from John O'Groats on the north coast of Scotland to Land's End in the south-west corner of England?**
A Approximately 1,100 miles (1,770 kilometres)
B Approximately 500 miles (800 kilometres)
C Approximately 870 miles (1,400 kilometres)
D Approximately 1,310 miles (2,110 kilometres)

53 **Where is the Scouse dialect spoken?**
A Cornwall
B London
C Liverpool
D Tyneside

54 **Where is the Cockney dialect spoken?**
A London
B Cornwall
C Tyneside
D Liverpool

55 **Where is the Geordie dialect spoken?**
- A Tyneside
- B Cornwall
- C Liverpool
- D London

56 **What other regional language, in addition to English, is also spoken in Scotland?**
- A French
- B Welsh
- C Gaelic
- D Scottish

57 **What percentage of London's population is made up of ethnic minorities?**
- A 45% of London's population
- B 29% of London's population
- C 9% of London's population
- D 15% of London's population

58 **Scots is the name of the old Scottish language. Is this statement true or false?**
- A False
- B True

59 **Which country of the UK has the highest proportion of ethnic minority groups in its population?**
- A Scotland
- B England
- C Northern Ireland
- D Wales

60 **According to the 2001 Census, what percentage of people stated their religion as Muslim?**

A Approximately 21%

B Approximately 1%

C Approximately 3%

D Approximately 15%

61 **Everyone in the UK has the legal right to practise the religion of their choice. Is this statement true or false?**

A True

B False

62 **What percentage of the UK population say they attend religious services?**

A Around 30%

B Around 20%

C Around 10%

D Around 40%

63 **According to the 2001 Census, what proportion of the UK population are Christians?**

A Two people out of ten

B Seven people out of ten

C Five people out of ten

D Nine people out of ten

64 **According to the 2001 Census, what percentage of the UK population reported that they had a religion?**
A   65%
B   75%
C   35%
D   55%

65 **When is the national day for Scotland?**
A   1 March
B   23 April
C   30 November
D   17 March

66 **What is the population of Scotland?**
A   1.3 million
B   5.1 million
C   3.2 million
D   7.8 million

67 **One of the dialects spoken in Northern Ireland is called Ulster Scots. Is this statement true or false?**
A   False
B   True

68 **Why was a census not carried out in the United Kingdom in 1941?**
A   No census was planned for that year
B   Because it was boycotted by the public
C   Because Britain was at war
D   Because it was abolished by the government

69 What is the population of Northern Ireland?
   A   0.9 million
   B   2.5 million
   C   3.1 million
   D   1.7 million

70 What is the population of England?
   A   About 60 million
   B   About 50 million
   C   About 40 million
   D   About 30 million

71 What is the population of Wales?
   A   2.9 million
   B   5.3 million
   C   1.2 million
   D   3.4 million

72 What is the estimated population of the United Kingdom?
   A   About 60 million
   B   About 50 million
   C   About 80 million
   D   About 40 million

73 What percentage of the UK's population lives in England?
   A   53%
   B   68%
   C   84%
   D   75%

74 **Over the last 20 years, there has been a decline in population in the north east and north west of England. Is this statement true or false?**

A False

B True

75 **What percentage of the UK's ethnic minorities live in the London area?**

A 14%

B 60%

C 30%

D 45%

76 **What is the second largest religious group in the UK?**

A Jewish

B Buddhist

C Sikh

D Muslim

77 **What is a census?**

A The government department that collects statistics

B A traditional English festival

C A form required for postal voting

D A count of the whole population

78 **What is the name of the patron saint of Scotland?**

  A St Patrick

  B St George

  C St Andrew

  D St David

79 **How often is a census carried out in the United Kingdom?**

  A Whenever the government decides

  B Once every eight years

  C Once every five years

  D Once every ten years

80 **In which year will the next UK census be carried out?**

  A 2008

  B 2011

  C 2015

  D 2020

81 **When was the first census carried out in the United Kingdom?**

  A 1801

  B 1785

  C 1851

  D 1912

82 **How many years must have passed before an individual's census form is viewable by the public?**

A 10 years

B 50 years

C 100 years

D An individual's census form is confidential and never viewable by the public

83 **What percentage of the UK population is made up of ethnic minorities?**

A About 2%

B About 8%

C About 15%

D About 25%

84 **How might you stop young people playing tricks on you at Hallowe'en?**

A Give them sweets or chocolates

B Give them some money

C Call the police

D Hide from them

85 **What is the name of the patron saint of England?**

A St Andrew

B St David

C St George

D St Patrick

86 When is New Year's Day?
A 1 March
B 1 January
C 25 December
D 31 December

87 When is Valentine's Day?
A 14 February
B 1 February
C 14 April
D 1 April

88 What do people sometimes do on Valentine's Day?
A Wear poppies in memory of St Valentine
B Fast from eating for the whole day
C Play jokes on each other until midday
D Send anonymous cards to someone they secretly admire

89 What traditionally happens on April Fool's Day?
A It is a public holiday until noon
B People play jokes on each other
C People enjoy public firework displays
D None of the above

90 When is April Fool's Day?
A 1 April
B 1 February
C 1 March
D 1 May

91 **What traditionally happens on Mother's Day?**
- A   People honour the mother of Jesus Christ
- B   People hold firework displays
- C   Mothers make special meals for their families
- D   People give cards or gifts to their mothers

92 **When is Christmas celebrated?**
- A   25 November
- B   1 January
- C   24 December
- D   25 December

93 **When is Hallowe'en celebrated?**
- A   31 October
- B   1 March
- C   1 November
- D   30 November

94 **What does Christmas Day celebrate?**
- A   The miracles of Jesus Christ
- B   The birth of Jesus Christ
- C   The resurrection of Jesus Christ
- D   The death of Jesus Christ

95 **When is Guy Fawkes Night?**
- A   The evening of 15 October
- B   The evening of 30 May
- C   The evening of 5 November
- D   The evening of 25 September

96 What does Guy Fawkes Night commemorate?
   A   Remembrance of those killed during war
   B   The invention of fireworks
   C   The failure of a plot to bomb Parliament
   D   The rebuilding of the Houses of Parliament

97 What do people wear on Remembrance Day in memory of those who have died at war?
   A   Poppies
   B   Black clothing
   C   Military clothing
   D   Red ribbons

98 When is Remembrance Day?
   A   31 August
   B   21 October
   C   11 November
   D   1 May

99 What does Remembrance Day commemorate?
   A   The crucifixion of Jesus Christ
   B   The appreciation of single mothers
   C   The celebration of community
   D   The memory of those who died fighting in wars

100 What is the Grand National?
   A   A golf championship
   B   A football cup
   C   A horse race
   D   A tennis tournament

101 **When is Mother's Day?**
- A The Sunday four weeks before Easter
- B The Saturday four weeks before Easter
- C The Sunday one week before Easter
- D The Sunday three weeks before Easter

102 **Which Christian denomination does the Church of Scotland belong to?**
- A Episcopal
- B Anglican
- C Roman Catholic
- D Presbyterian

103 **What is the name of the patron saint of Northern Ireland?**
- A St George
- B St Andrew
- C St David
- D St Patrick

104 **When is the national day for Wales?**
- A 30 November
- B 23 April
- C 1 March
- D 17 March

105 **What is the name of the patron saint of Wales?**
- A St George
- B St Andrew
- C St Patrick
- D St David

106 When is the national day for Northern Ireland?
A   17 March
B   1 March
C   30 November
D   23 April

107 The Queen must not marry anyone who is not Protestant. Is this statement true or false?
A   True
B   False

108 How is the Archbishop of Canterbury selected?
A   The selection is made by a vote in the House of Lords
B   The selection is made by public referendum
C   The monarch makes the selection based on the choice of the Prime Minister and a committee appointed by the Church of England
D   The monarch makes the selection based on the choice of the outgoing Archbishop of Canterbury

109 Which other name can be used to refer to the Church of England?
A   The Methodist Church
B   The Catholic Church
C   The Presbyterian Church
D   The Anglican Church

110 **What is traditionally eaten on Christmas Day?**

    A   Roast pork and trifle

    B   Turkey

    C   Poached salmon

    D   Beer battered cod and chips

111 **The Church of England is called the Episcopal Church in Scotland. Is this statement true or false?**

    A   True

    B   False

112 **What sport is played at the Wimbledon tournament?**

    A   Rugby

    B   Tennis

    C   Football

    D   Cricket

113 **When did the Church of England come into existence?**

    A   In the 1640s

    B   In the 1530s

    C   In the 1440s

    D   In the 1750s

114 **Who is the monarch not allowed to marry?**

    A   Anyone who is not of royal blood

    B   Anyone who is under the age of 25

    C   Anyone who was born outside the UK

    D   Anyone who is not Protestant

115 Which of the UK national days is celebrated with a public holiday?

A   St Patrick's Day in Northern Ireland

B   St Andrew's Day in Scotland

C   St George's Day in England

D   St David's Day in Wales

116 Which of these statements is correct?

A   Boxing Day and New Year are both public holidays

B   New Year is a public holiday and Boxing Day is not

117 When is Boxing Day?

A   26 December

B   25 December

C   31 December

D   1 January

118 What is the title of the King or Queen within the Church of England?

A   Head Priest

B   Supreme Governor

C   Archbishop of Canterbury

D   Governor General

CHAPTER 3: HOW THE UNITED KINGDOM IS GOVERNED

This chapter maps out the detail of government structures in the United Kingdom. Many would argue that this is the chapter that applicants find most difficult to learn. And those same people would probably say that the questions drawn from this chapter are some of the most obscure. All elements of Britain's complex mix of administrative institutions and traditions are captured. From the basics of local government up to the relative mysteries of the European Commission, all are included in some detail. Questions on national government are primarily focused on roles: the voter, the media, the Queen, the Prime Minister, the devolved administrations – all are likely to be dealt with. And all must be considered in the context of Britain's unwritten constitution. Also tested are the rules for standing for election, whether it be at a local, national or European level.

Finally, the chapter sets out the position of Britain in international affairs. Primarily discussed are the Commonwealth, the United Nations and the European Union. The details of how the various European institutions work are particularly challenging to grasp.

Questions from this chapter tend to stretch even the most confident of applicants. Be warned. Anyone who doesn't have a working day-to-day knowledge of how democracy is carried out in this country is going to find questions from this chapter exceptionally tough. And questions about the operation of the European Union may stump even the most knowledgeable.

119 **In which year were the Assembly for Wales and the Scottish Parliament created?**

A 1982

B 1969

C 1972

D 1999

120 **How many politicians are there in the Cabinet?**

A About 30

B About 40

C About 20

D About 10

121 **What is the role of the Cabinet?**

A To provide royal assent for new laws

B To make decisions about government policy

C To examine laws proposed by the House of Commons

D To investigate serious complaints against the police

122 Which minister can sit in the House of Lords or in the House of Commons?

- A Foreign Secretary
- B Home Secretary
- C Lord Chancellor
- D Chancellor of the Exchequer

123 What is the second largest party in the House of Commons called?

- A The Opposition
- B The Cabinet
- C The Government
- D The Shadow Cabinet

124 Which politicians are members of the Shadow Cabinet?

- A The remaining MPs in Government who are not in the Cabinet
- B Peers from the House of Lords
- C Senior members of the main opposition party
- D Civil servants working for the government

125 What are the functions of the Speaker of the House of Commons? Select two options from below

- A To give royal assent to new laws agreed in the House of Commons
- B To keep order during political debates
- C To make sure rules are followed in the House of Commons
- D To promote members from the House of Commons to the House of Lords

126 **How is the Speaker of the House of Commons chosen?**
- A Elected by the public
- B Chosen by the Prime Minister
- C Appointed by the King or Queen
- D Elected by fellow MPs

127 **There are no independent MPs in Parliament. Is this statement true or false?**
- A True
- B False

128 **Someone is more likely to be elected as an MP if they have been nominated to represent a major political party. Is this statement true or false?**
- A True
- B False

129 **What are two key features of the civil service? Select two options from below**
- A Business knowledge
- B Party loyalty
- C Political neutrality
- D Professionalism

130 **What is a civil servant?**
- A A manager or administrator who works for the House of Lords
- B A manager or administrator who carries out government policy
- C A member of a political party
- D A Member of Parliament

131 **Which policy areas have not been transferred to the Welsh Assembly or the Scottish Parliament and remain under central UK government control? Select two options from below**

A Defence

B Education

C Foreign affairs

D Health

132 **Which country does not have its own parliament or national assembly?**

A Northern Ireland

B Scotland

C England

D Wales

133 **What is the name of the ministerial position that is responsible for the economy?**

A Home Secretary

B Chancellor of the Exchequer

C Chief Whip

D Lord Chancellor

134 **Which of the following parliaments or assemblies use proportional representation?**

A European Parliament

B Northern Ireland Assembly

C Scottish Parliament

D All of the above

135 **Which one of the following parliaments or assemblies does not use proportional representation?**

A House of Commons

B Scottish Parliament

C Welsh Assembly

D Northern Ireland Assembly

136 **Which voting system is used to elect the Scottish Parliament and the Welsh Assembly?**

A A ranking or preferential system

B Assembly members are chosen by the government

C Proportional representation

D "First past the post"

137 **On which matters can the Welsh Assembly make decisions? Select two options from below**

A Defence

B Environment

C Foreign policy

D Transport

138 **Where is the National Assembly for Wales situated?**

A Swansea

B Cardiff

C Stormont

D Edinburgh

139 **Where does the Scottish Parliament sit?**

A Edinburgh

B Aberdeen

C Stormont

D Glasgow

140 **On which matters can the Scottish Parliament make decisions? Select two options from below**

A Defence

B Education

C Foreign policy

D Health

141 **The Scottish Parliament has powers to raise additional tax. Is this statement true or false?**

A True

B False

142 **When was the Northern Ireland Parliament established?**

A 1945

B 1938

C 1956

D 1922

143 **What type of constitution does the UK have?**

A An unwritten constitution

B An amended constitution

C A written constitution

D A legal constitution

144 **When did the government start a programme of devolved administration for Wales and Scotland?**

A   1982

B   1997

C   1979

D   2001

145 **What are the roles of the Whips in Parliament? Select two correct roles from below**

A   Ensure attendance of MPs at voting time in the House of Commons

B   Ensure the House of Commons is always safe and secure

C   Keep order in the House of Commons during political debates

D   Responsible for discipline in their party

146 **Who is the Head of State of the United Kingdom?**

A   The Home Secretary

B   The Speaker of the House of Commons

C   The King or Queen

D   The Prime Minister

147 **The monarch rules the UK and can reject laws and decisions made by government and the Cabinet. Is this statement true or false?**

A   False

B   True

148 Who is the current heir to the throne?
- A The Duke of Edinburgh
- B The Duke of York
- C The Prince of Wales
- D Prince William

149 Which of the following is an important ceremonial role that the King or Queen performs?
- A Meeting weekly with the Prime Minister
- B Opening of a new parliamentary session
- C Voting in the House of Commons
- D Chairing proceedings in the House of Lords

150 When are general elections held?
- A At least every year
- B At least every four years
- C At least every five years
- D At least every ten years

151 Which of these statements is correct?
- A Prime Minister's Questions take place every fortnight all year round
- B Prime Minister's Questions take place every week when Parliament is sitting

152 Which of these statements is correct?
- A The House of Commons is the more important of the two chambers in Parliament
- B The House of Lords is the more important of the two chambers in Parliament

153 **The Prime Minister and most members of the Cabinet are MPs. Is this statement true or false?**

A   False

B   True

154 **What is the name of the system that governs how MPs are elected into the House of Commons?**

A   Electoral college system

B   Proportional representation system

C   "First past the post" system

D   Aggregated vote system

155 **What must a candidate achieve in order to win their constituency?**

A   Win the most votes out of all candidates in their constituency

B   Win at least 15,000 votes

C   Be a member of the party that wins government office

D   Win at least 25% of the votes within their constituency

156 **What is the name of the ministerial position that is responsible for legal affairs?**

A   Foreign Secretary

B   Home Secretary

C   Lord Chancellor

D   Chancellor of the Exchequer

157 **The House of Commons cannot overrule the decisions of the House of Lords. Is this statement true or false?**
A True
B False

158 **The UK government cannot suspend the Northern Ireland Assembly. Is this statement true or false?**
A True
B False

159 **What is the name of the ministerial position that is responsible for law, order and immigration?**
A Home Secretary
B Chief Whip
C Lord Chancellor
D Chancellor of the Exchequer

160 **Which of the following are important roles of the Prime Minister? Select two options from below**
A Appoint the members of the Cabinet
B Effect new laws by giving royal assent to legislation
C Leader of the party in power
D Perform the duties of Head of State

161 Where is the Prime Minister's official residence?

A 10 Downing Street

B 12 Downing Street

C Palace of Westminster

D Buckingham Palace

162 What is the role of a Member of Parliament? Select two options from below

A Elect members of the House of Lords

B Represent their constituency

C Scrutinise and comment on what the government is doing

D Vote in the European Parliament

163 A Prime Minister can be removed from office by their party at any time. Is this statement true or false?

A True

B False

164 How is it decided which party forms the government?

A The party with the most votes forms the government

B The party with the most candidates forms the government

C The party that wins the majority of constituencies forms the government

D The members of the House of Lords vote for their preferred party

165 **What are the functions of the House of Lords? Select two options from below**

A   Elect the Prime Minister

B   Elect the Speaker of the House of Commons

C   Propose new laws

D   Suggest amendments to laws

166 **How are Whips appointed?**

A   By the Prime Minister

B   By vote amongst their peers

C   By the King or Queen

D   By their party leaders

167 **Hereditary peers have lost the automatic right to attend the House of Lords. Is this statement true or false?**

A   True

B   False

168 **What is a Life Peer?**

A   A member of the House of Lords who has been appointed by the Prime Minister

B   A hereditary aristocrat or peer of the realm

C   Any person who has inherited a peerage from their family

D   Any person who has served as an MP for more than 20 years

169 In what year did the Prime Minister gain powers to nominate members of the House of Lords?

A 1980
B 1968
C 1973
D 1958

170 How often are elections for the European Parliament held?

A Every four years
B Every ten years
C Every year
D Every five years

171 Where can you read copies of Hansard? Select two options from below

A Newspapers
B Television
C Large libraries
D Internet

172 The "first past the post" system is used to elect members of the European Parliament. Is this statement true or false?

A True
B False

173 How often does the Cabinet normally meet?

A Monthly
B Bi-weekly
C Daily
D Weekly

174 **What is the name of the country house of the Prime Minister?**

A   10 Downing Street

B   Balmoral Castle

C   Palace of Westminster

D   Chequers

175 **EU citizens living in the UK can vote in general elections. Is this statement true or false?**

A   True

B   False

176 **Which of these statements is correct?**

A   Citizens of the European Union must always have a valid work permit to work in any EU member state

B   Subject to some restrictions, citizens of the European Union have the right to work in any EU member state

177 **How can you get tickets to listen to debates at the Houses of Parliament? Select two answers from below**

A   Write to your local MP

B   Queue at the public entrance

C   Book tickets online

D   Buy them from nearby ticket outlets

178 **What is the current minimum age for standing for public office?**

A   18 years
B   25 years
C   30 years
D   21 years

179 **What may prevent you from being able to stand for public office? Select two options from below**

A   Being a citizen of the Irish Republic
B   Being a Commonwealth citizen
C   Being a member of the armed forces
D   Having been found guilty of a criminal offence

180 **What must a candidate have in order to become a local councillor?**

A   A connection with the area in which they wish to take office
B   A deposit of £500
C   Membership of a political party
D   A recommendation from their local MP

181 **Members of the public are not able to visit the Houses of Parliament. Is this statement true or false?**

A   True
B   False

182 **How many member states are there in the Commonwealth?**
- A   25 member states
- B   75 member states
- C   39 member states
- D   53 member states

183 **Who is the head of the Commonwealth?**
- A   The Secretary of the Commonwealth
- B   The Archbishop of Canterbury
- C   The Queen
- D   The British Prime Minister

184 **When did the UK join the European Union?**
- A   1935
- B   1959
- C   1973
- D   The UK is not a member of the European Union

185 **How many countries are members of the European Union?**
- A   15 countries
- B   12 countries
- C   41 countries
- D   27 countries

186 **How often is the electoral register updated?**
- A   Every five years
- B   Every year
- C   Every two years
- D   Every time somebody moves house

187 **What is the main aim behind the European Union today?**

A   For member states to function as a single market

B   For member states to protect human rights in Europe

C   For member states to observe a single set of laws

D   For member states to improve efficiency

188 **Where is the European Commission based?**

A   Brussels

B   Geneva

C   Paris

D   Strasbourg

189 **The Council of Ministers, together with the European Parliament, is the legislative body of the European Union. Is this statement true or false?**

A   True

B   False

190 **What is the role of the European Commission? Select two options from below**

A   Administer EU funding programmes

B   Draft proposals for new EU policies and laws

C   Select the members of the Council of Ministers

D   Select the members of the European Parliament

191 What is a role of the European Parliament?
- A Ensure EU regulations and directives are being followed by member states
- B Review European court cases that have been appealed
- C Examine decisions made by the European Council and the European Commission
- D Elect individual members of the European Commission

192 European Union law is legally binding in the UK. Is this statement true or false?
- A True
- B False

193 The UK is a member of the European Union but not of the Council of Europe. Is this statement true or false?
- A True
- B False

194 What is the purpose of the Council of Europe?
- A To debate proposals, decisions and expenditure of the European Commission
- B To create a single market for members of the council
- C To develop conventions which focus on human rights, democracy, education, the environment, health and culture
- D To create new European regulations and directives

195 **A country cannot be expelled from the Council of Europe. Is this statement true or false?**

A True

B False

196 **The Council of Europe has no power to make laws. Is this statement true or false?**

A True

B False

197 **When was the Council of Europe established?**

A 1964

B 1901

C 1982

D 1949

198 **What is the purpose of the United Nations?**

A To create global laws to regulate foreign affairs

B To create a single market for all world nations

C To debate global third world development and funding proposals

D To prevent war and promote international peace and security

199 **What is the United Kingdom's role within the United Nations?**
- A Member of the UN Security Council
- B Selects the UN Secretary General from members of the Security Council
- C Provides a neutral location for hosting UN meetings in Scotland
- D All of the above

200 **Britain was a founding member of the EU. Is this statement true or false?**
- A True
- B False

201 **Non-departmental public bodies are under the political control of the government. Is this statement true or false?**
- A True
- B False

202 **Where do local authorities get most of their funding from?**
- A Government taxation
- B Local Council Tax
- C Lottery grants
- D Issuing parking tickets

203 **All candidates standing for office in local government must be members of a political party. Is this statement true or false?**
- A True
- B False

204 **A judge can order a public body to change its practices or pay compensation if it is not respecting a person's human rights. Is this statement true or false?**

A True

B False

205 **Can a judge change an Act of Parliament if it is incompatible with the Human Rights Act?**

A Yes, but they must seek the Prime Minister's approval first

B Yes, but only if they believe the law is unfair

C Yes, but they must obtain permission from the Lord Chancellor

D No, but they can ask Parliament to consider doing so

206 **Which of these statements is correct?**

A A judge can decide whether a person is guilty or innocent of a serious crime

B A judge can only decide on the penalty for a person found guilty of a serious crime

207 **When can a magistrate decide whether a person is guilty or innocent?**

A   If a person is accused of having committed a minor crime

B   A magistrate can always decide whether a person is guilty or innocent regardless of the alleged crime

C   If a person is accused of having committed a serious crime

D   A magistrate cannot decide whether a person is guilty or innocent; instead a jury must always be used

208 **When is a jury used?**

A   To choose an appropriate penalty for someone found guilty of a serious crime

B   To confirm decisions made by a judge

C   To decide if someone is innocent or guilty of a less important crime

D   To decide if someone is innocent or guilty of a serious crime

209 **What is the name of the largest police force in the United Kingdom?**

A   Humberside Police

B   The Bill

C   Merseyside Police

D   The Metropolitan Police

210 **Who is responsible for investigating serious complaints against the police?**
A The Home Secretary
B The Police Commissioner
C The Independent Police Complaints Commission
D The Lord Chancellor

211 **Members of the House of Lords can stand for election to the House of Commons. Is this statement true or false?**
A True
B False

212 **Which of the following statements is correct about political reporting during election periods in the UK? Select two options from below**
A All reporting on radio and television must be balanced
B It is illegal for newspapers to run campaigns to influence people's opinions
C Politicians must be able to read interview questions beforehand
D Television channels have to give equal time to rival viewpoints

213 **How do you register to vote?**
- A Bring your passport to any polling booth on election day
- B Contact your local MP's office
- C Do nothing – all eligible citizens are automatically registered
- D Contact your local council election registration office

214 **In which elections can European citizens vote? Select two answers from below**
- A Elections to the House of Lords
- B European elections
- C Local elections
- D National elections

215 **Voter registration forms are available in several languages. Is this statement true or false?**
- A True
- B False

216 **Which of these statements is correct?**
- A Both UK born and naturalised citizens have the right to vote
- B Only UK born citizens have the right to vote

217 The Government has the power to instruct the police to follow its instructions on what to do in a particular case. Is this statement true or false?

A   True
B   False

218 When was the current voting age set?

A   1969
B   1945
C   1982
D   1956

219 Which of these statements is correct?

A   The Metropolitan Police is based at New Scotland Yard
B   The Metropolitan Police is based in the Palace of Westminster

220 Newspaper owners and editors do not try to influence public opinion. Is this statement true or false?

A   True
B   False

221 Newspapers cannot publish political opinions or run campaigns to influence government. Is this statement true or false?

A   True
B   False

222 **Which of these statements is correct?**
   A   Proceedings in Parliament are never made public
   B   Proceedings in Parliament are publicly available

223 **What is the name of the official record of proceedings in Parliament?**
   A   Parliament News
   B   Hansard
   C   Westminster Hour
   D   The Recorder

224 **What is a quango?**
   A   The name of the British citizenship ceremony
   B   A non-departmental public body
   C   Another name for the Lord Chancellor
   D   A local police officer

225 **It is not possible to see the electoral register as this would damage the privacy of voters. Is this statement true or false?**
   A   True
   B   False

226 **What is the current voting age?**
   A   21 years old
   B   20 years old
   C   16 years old
   D   18 years old

CHAPTER 4: EVERYDAY NEEDS

In theory this is the chapter that people living in Britain today should find the most familiar. And, as such, the questions from the chapter should be straightforward. The contents of the chapter are essentially a brief guide to how to
get by in this country in terms of everyday activities, such
as accessing key services and dealing with major public
and private organisations. Housing is a key area. Whether
it be renting or buying, all the ins and outs of the process
must be known, such as dealing with estate agents, solici-
tors, housing associations and local authorities.

Money is another area covered, and you must understand the roles of key financial organisations. The NHS is
generally regarded as a national treasure. But for a new-
comer, understanding how to access health services can
be a challenge. You will need to know how to find a doc-
tor, get registered and then get access to the various services available, from dentists to maternity services.

Questions will also cover the various stages of education available in this country. A complex area that is often
asked about in the citizenship test is that of assessment.
You will need to know about key stages and when children must take the exams that are associated with the
various stages. Given that these vary between the countries of the United Kingdom, this can get tricky.

Difficult questions from this chapter often relate to the
rules and regulations relating to the pursuit of leisure in

the United Kingdom. Detailed questions are likely on the ratings system that applies to films, the television licensing system, laws on consumption of alcohol and gambling restrictions. Finally, the chapter sets out the complex set of rules, customs and laws that apply to private and public transport.

There is a great deal in this chapter that can be asked about. A lot of it is what you probably already know, but a large amount is probably what you most likely should already know, but don't.

227 How is the NHS Direct service provided?

    A Over the telephone

    B Using a mobile surgery or ambulance

    C At your GP's surgery

    D At your nearest hospital

228 Which of these statements is correct?

    A If you lose your cash or debit card you must inform the bank immediately

    B If you lose your cash or debit card you should only inform the bank if you are sure it has been stolen

229 What do you need to provide to open a bank account? Select two options from below

    A £500

    B A work permit

    C Proof of your address

    D Proof of your identity

230 **Foreign currency can only be bought or changed at post offices. Is this statement true or false?**
A True
B False

231 **People borrowing money from banks to pay for cars and holidays is more common in the UK than in many other countries. Is this statement true or false?**
A True
B False

232 **What denomination of bank notes does not exist in the UK?**
A £2
B £5
C £50
D £20

233 **Which of these statements is correct?**
A Banks only take your previous credit record into account when making a decision about a loan
B If you are refused a loan you have the right to ask the reason why

234 **Who should you speak to if you have trouble with your neighbours? Select two options from below**

A The bank

B The local authority

C Your GP

D Your landlord

235 **What age must you be to be allowed into betting shops or gambling clubs?**

A 15 years old

B 16 years old

C 17 years old

D 18 years old

236 **If only one person lives in a house how much reduction do they get on their Council Tax?**

A 25%

B 50%

C 75%

D 5%

237 **If you are the tenant of a property then you do not have to pay Council Tax. Is this statement true or false?**

A True

B False

238 **How are local government services paid for? Select two options from below**
- A Charitable donations
- B Council Tax
- C Grants from central government
- D Insurance premiums

239 **In Northern Ireland there is a system of domestic rates instead of Council Tax. Is this statement true or false?**
- A True
- B False

240 **When did 12 European states adopt the euro as a common currency?**
- A 1995
- B 2002
- C 2000
- D 1980

241 **Which of the following statements is correct?**
- A If you need to see a specialist for medical treatment then you must see your GP first
- B You should always go directly to a specialist if you believe you know the medical treatment you require

242 **What proportion of people in the UK own their own home?**
A One-third
B One-quarter
C Two-thirds
D Half

243 **Who is given priority when GPs visit patients at home?**
A Older people
B Pregnant women
C Children under five years old
D People who are unable to travel

244 **If you cannot find a GP, who can you ask for help to find one?**
A The local hospital
B Your local MP
C The local health authority
D Citizens Advice Bureau

245 **When should you look for a GP?**
A Once you have registered with the local authority
B When you become ill
C As soon as you move to a new area
D When you visit the local hospital

246 **What will happen if you do not pay the total amount of your monthly credit card bill?**

A   You will be unable to use the card until the bill is paid

B   You will be required to return the card to the credit card company

C   You will be charged interest

D   Nothing

247 **Which of these statements is correct?**

A   If you have a dispute with your neighbour then you may be able to avoid going to court by using a mediator

B   If you have a dispute with your neighbour then you can only resolve it by going to court

248 **Which phone numbers should be called in an emergency for police, fire and ambulance services? Select two options from below**

A   111

B   112

C   911

D   999

249 **Which of these statements is correct?**

A   General Practitioners always work together in group practices

B   Group practices of General Practitioners are sometimes called Primary Health Care Centres

250 **What does NHS stand for?**
- A National Hockey Stadium
- B National Health Service
- C New Homes Show
- D National Horse Show

251 **Who are welfare benefits not available to?**
- A The unemployed
- B People who do not have legal rights of residence in the UK
- C The elderly
- D The sick and disabled

252 **You need an appointment to visit an NHS walk-in centre. Is this statement true or false?**
- A True
- B False

253 **Where can you get further information about welfare benefits? Select two answers from below**
- A A bank
- B A building society
- C Citizens Advice Bureau
- D Jobcentre Plus

254 **Insurance for a car or motorcycle is optional. Is this statement true or false?**
- A True
- B False

255 **Which of these statements is correct?**
  A In an emergency you can attend a hospital, but only if you have a letter from your GP
  B In an emergency you should go to the Accident and Emergency department of your nearest hospital

256 **Which of the following statements is correct?**
  A Everyone is entitled to apply for council accommodation
  B Only people on benefits are entitled to apply for council accommodation

257 **What is housing provided by local authorities often called?**
  A Free housing
  B Market housing
  C Local housing
  D Council housing

258 **Who will provide the legal agreements necessary for you to buy a home?**
  A The local authority
  B A solicitor
  C A bank
  D A surveyor

259 **When buying a home in Scotland, a survey is carried out before making an offer. Is this statement true or false?**

A True

B False

260 **Who is responsible for the collection of refuse?**

A The local authority

B The police

C The NHS

D Your landlord

261 **When you make an offer on a home you want to buy, who is this usually done through? Select two answers from below**

A A bank

B A GP

C A solicitor

D An estate agent

262 **Which statement is correct?**

A When you agree to buy a home you sign a tenancy agreement or lease

B When you rent a home privately you sign a tenancy agreement or lease

263 **When you make an offer on a home you want to buy, why must the offer be "subject to contract"?**

A So that you can withdraw if there are reasons you cannot complete the purchase

B So the seller can check if they can get a better offer elsewhere

C So the local authority can review the offer

D So the purchase can be completed as quickly as possible

264 **Estate agents represent the person buying a house or flat. Is this statement true or false?**

A True

B False

265 **Which two places can you get visits from or meet with a Health Visitor?**

A In your home

B At a clinic

C At a nursery school

D In your local community centre

266 **Where can you get a mortgage from? Select two correct answers from below**

A A bank

B A building society

C A housing association

D An estate agent

267 People in the UK who buy their own home usually pay for it with a mortgage. Is this statement true or false?

A True

B False

268 Who carries out checks on a house that you want to buy?

A A landlord

B A housing association

C The seller

D A surveyor

269 A tenancy agreement will be for a fixed period of time. Is this statement true or false?

A True

B False

270 It is not possible to choose between electricity and gas suppliers. Is this statement true or false?

A True

B False

271 At what voltage is electricity supplied to homes in the UK?

A 50 volts

B 110 volts

C 240 volts

D 1000 volts

272 **In Northern Ireland the cost of water supply is included in domestic rates. Is this statement true or false?**
- A True
- B False

273 **What is the charge for the supply of water to a home called?**
- A Supply rates
- B Piping charge
- C Income tax
- D Water rates

274 **If you are having problems with your landlord where can you go for help and advice? Select two options from below**
- A A Primary Health Care Centre
- B Citizens Advice Bureau
- C DVLA
- D The housing department of the local authority

275 **In many areas of the UK there is a shortage of council accommodation. Is this statement true or false?**
- A True
- B False

276 **A tenant must leave a home if the landlord has a court order requiring the tenant to do so. Is this statement true or false?**
A True
B False

277 **Housing associations are run by the government. Is this statement true or false?**
A True
B False

278 **What is the purpose of Housing Benefit?**
A To help you sell a home
B To help you fix a home
C To help you pay your rent
D To help you buy a home

279 **Choose the correct statement from below**
A A landlord can raise the rent, but only one month after the tenancy agreement has been signed
B After a tenancy agreement has been signed, a landlord cannot raise the rent without agreement from the tenant

280 **Why will you be asked to give a landlord a deposit at the beginning of your tenancy?**
A To pay for electricity supply at the property
B To cover the cost of any damage to the property
C To pay for keys to the property
D To start a bank account

281 **A deposit paid to the landlord at the beginning of a tenancy is usually equal to one month's rent. Is this statement true or false?**
  A   True
  B   False

282 **What is contained in an inventory, when one is attached to a tenancy agreement?**
  A   A list of all furniture and fittings in a property
  B   A list of all people who have lived in a property
  C   Information about the owner of a property
  D   A record of the rent paid for a property

283 **If you do not pay your electricity bill and the supply is cut off, you can be reconnected for free. Is this statement true or false?**
  A   True
  B   False

284 **Where should you go for help if you are homeless?**
  A   To the local authority
  B   To the local hospital
  C   To your GP
  D   To your MP

285 **What is the role of the National Trust?**
  A Preserve important buildings and countryside in the UK
  B Guarantee a pension for government employees
  C Collect the TV licence fee
  D Maintain and enhance the residence of the Prime Minister

286 **You always have to pay a charge to receive treatment from your GP. Is this statement true or false?**
  A True
  B False

287 **All dogs in public places must wear a collar showing the name and address of the owner. Is this statement true or false?**
  A True
  B False

288 **What is the standard closing time of a pub?**
  A 1am
  B 11pm
  C 2am
  D 10pm

289 **Somebody aged 16 can drink wine or beer with a meal in a hotel or restaurant. Is this statement true or false?**
  A True
  B False

290 **All taxis and minicabs must be licensed and display a licence plate. Is this statement true or false?**

A True

B False

291 **What is the minimum age to be able to drink alcohol in a pub?**

A 16 years old

B 21 years old

C 18 years old

D It depends if you are with an adult

292 **What is the minimum age required to drive a car?**

A 17 years old

B 16 years old

C 18 years old

D 21 years old

293 **People have to buy a TV licence for each individual TV they own. Is this statement true or false?**

A True

B False

294 What does the film classification U mean?

A No one under 18 is allowed to see or rent the film

B Suitable for everyone but some parts of the film might be unsuitable for children

C Suitable for anyone aged four years or over

D Children under 15 are not allowed to see or rent the film

295 Which of these statements is correct?

A No one younger than 18 may see an 18-rated film under any circumstances

B No one younger than 18 may see an 18-rated film unless they are with an adult

296 What does the film classification PG mean?

A Suitable for everyone but some parts of the film might be unsuitable for children

B No one under 18 is allowed to see or rent the film

C Children under 15 are not allowed to see or rent the film

D Suitable for anyone aged four years or over

297 University students in England, Wales and Northern Ireland do not have to pay tuition fees. Is this statement true or false?

A True

B False

298 **What are courses for people who want to improve their English language skills called?**

A   NHS

B   EEE

C   ESOL

D   EAL

299 **Your car insurance will not be valid if you do not have a valid MOT certificate. Is this statement true or false?**

A   True

B   False

300 **When are you likely to be required to prove your identity? Select two options from below**

A   When applying for Housing Benefit

B   When opening a bank account

C   When purchasing National Rail tickets

D   When travelling between England and Wales

301 **What should you do if you are involved in a road accident? Select two options from below**

A   Admit that the accident was your fault

B   Exchange driving licences with the other driver

C   Give your details to the other driver

D   Make a note of everything that happened and contact your insurance company

302 You cannot be arrested if you refuse to take a breathalyser test. Is this statement true or false?

    A True

    B False

303 What is the speed limit for cars and motorcycles on single carriageways?

    A 80 miles per hour

    B 70 miles per hour

    C 90 miles per hour

    D 60 miles per hour

304 What is the speed limit for cars and motorcycles on motorways and dual carriageways?

    A 70 miles per hour

    B 50 miles per hour

    C 100 miles per hour

    D 60 miles per hour

305 Which of these statements is correct?

    A Tickets for trains are usually bought before you get on the train

    B Tickets for trains are usually bought when you have reached your destination

306 How often are you required to take your vehicle for an MOT test if it is over three years old?

A Every five years

B You only need an MOT test if the car has been involved in an accident

C Every two years

D Every year

307 Parents are not allowed to sit on a school's governing body. Is this statement true or false?

A True

B False

308 Which of these statements is correct?

A It is a criminal offence to have a car without motor insurance

B It is not a criminal offence to have a car without motor insurance if you only drive it occasionally

309 If you have a driving licence from a country outside the EU, you may use it in the UK for up to 12 months. Is this statement true or false?

A True

B False

310 In Northern Ireland, a newly qualified driver must display an R-Plate for one year after passing the test. Is this statement true or false?

A True

B False

311 After the age of 70, drivers must renew their driving licence for three years at a time. Is this statement true or false?

A True

B False

312 What are two stages that you must complete before you can get a full driving licence? Choose two correct answers from below

A Pass a breathalyser test

B Pass a practical driving test

C Pass a written theory test

D Pass an MOT test

313 What is the speed limit for cars and motorcycles in built-up areas?

A 60 miles per hour

B 30 miles per hour

C 50 miles per hour

D 70 miles per hour

314 **At what age do children in Northern Ireland begin secondary school?**

A 9

B 11

C 12

D 15

315 **In primary schools boys and girls usually learn together. Is this statement true or false?**

A True

B False

316 **At what age can children in the UK choose to leave school?**

A 12

B 18

C 16

D 14

317 **Education in the UK is free and voluntary for children between the ages of 5 and 16. Is this statement true or false?**

A True

B False

318 **Which of the following people do not qualify for free prescriptions in England?**

A A 22-year-old university student

B A 15-year-old school boy

C A 45-year-old man receiving Income Support

D A 35-year-old mother with a baby under 12 months old

319 **What does the Family Planning Association provide advice on? Select two options from below**

A Ambulance services

B Contraception

C Family values

D Sexual heath

320 **At what age do children in Scotland go to secondary school?**

A 9

B 12

C 11

D 15

321 **Which of these statements is correct?**

A Antenatal care is only available from special private clinics and is not part of the NHS

B You can get regular antenatal care from your local hospital, local health centre or from special antenatal clinics

322 **In Scotland, eye tests are free. Is this statement true or false?**

A True

B False

323 **In Wales, free dental treatment is available to all people. Is this statement true or false?**

A True

B False

324 Which of these statements is correct?
  A All dentists work for the NHS
  B Some dentists have two sets of charges, both NHS and private

325 When you stay overnight in hospital you need to provide your own meals. Is this statement true or false?
  A True
  B False

326 What are you called if you need to stay overnight in hospital?
  A An outpatient
  B An in-patient
  C A day patient
  D A night patient

327 Within what period of time must a baby be registered with the Registrar of Births, Marriages and Deaths?
  A Six weeks
  B Twelve months
  C One week
  D Six months

328 How many independent schools are there in the UK?
  A 100
  B 1,000
  C 2,500
  D 15,000

329 **Which of these statements is correct?**

A   A driving licence or a recent phone bill may be used to prove your identity

B   An identity card is the only document that can be used to prove your identity

330 **In Wales, what is the name of the organisation that provides advice on careers to children from the age of 11?**

A   NHS Wales

B   Careers Wales

C   Wales Connections

D   Wales EAL

331 **In England careers advice for children aged 14 and over is available from Connexions. Is this statement true or false?**

A   True

B   False

332 **If your child's main language is not English they can get extra support from a specialist teacher. What is this teacher called?**

A   PAL teacher

B   ESE teacher

C   EAL teacher

D   LLL teacher

333 **At what ages are Key Stage Tests held in England?**
A 10, 12 and 14
B 7, 11 and 14
C 7 and 15
D 11, 15 and 17

334 **Which of these statements is correct?**
A Parents are allowed to withdraw their children from religious education lessons
B Schools can choose to provide religious education to pupils

335 **In Northern Ireland many secondary schools select children through a test taken at the age of 11. Is this statement true or false?**
A True
B False

336 **Independent schools are paid for by the state. Is this statement true or false?**
A True
B False

337 **At what age do children in England go to secondary school?**
A 9
B 11
C 12
D 15

338 **In Northern Ireland, what are schools that aim to bring children of different religions together called?**

A   Shared schools

B   Integrated schools

C   Joined schools

D   Faith schools

339 **Schools in the UK that are linked to a particular religion are called "faith schools". Is this statement true or false?**

A   True

B   False

340 **Secondary schools are smaller than primary schools. Is this statement true or false?**

A   True

B   False

341 **Who should you approach to get information about local secondary schools?**

A   Your local MP

B   NHS Direct

C   The local education authority

D   Your nearest school

342 **At what age do children in Wales go to secondary school?**

A   9

B   11

C   12

D   15

343 How many days a year must a school open?

 A 190 days

 B 365 days

 C 100 days

 D 150 days

344 What percentage of children in the UK attend independent schools?

 A About 8%

 B About 22%

 C About 40%

 D About 95%

CHAPTER 5: EMPLOYMENT

This chapter provides a wide array of information about working in Britain. The workplace is becoming an increasingly complex place as the government moves to make access to employment and opportunities as fair as possible. This, of course, creates rules, regulations and laws, and this is where many of the questions from this chapter focus.

The first part of the chapter provides useful advice about the process of looking for work. The next section focuses in much more detail on the laws and legal obligations that govern the workplace. These are complex and, while the principles involved will be familiar to many, the details may not. You can expect to be tested on a range of topics from tax and National Insurance obligations to redundancy pay and pension entitlements.

The final section of the chapter focuses on the interaction between families and the workplace. The intricate details of childcare provisions and parental leave allowances may be a mystery to many people. An area that may also be unfamiliar to some is the strict set of laws that apply to children who work. Overall, questions from this chapter may look somewhat unfamiliar to many British people. They may have been aware that rules and regulations in these areas of life existed, but to pass the citizenship test these have to be known.

345 **Everyone in the UK is allowed to work. Is this statement true or false?**
   A   True
   B   False

346 **Select the correct statement**
   A   Employers can employ anyone as long as they have a UK bank account
   B   Employers have to check that everyone they employ is legally entitled to work in the UK

347 **How can you compare qualifications from another country with those in the UK?**
   A   By visiting your local library
   B   By contacting the National Academic Recognition Information Centre
   C   By writing to potential employers
   D   By asking your neighbour

348 **What might you need to complete or provide when applying for a job? Select two options from below**
   A   A covering letter or letter of application
   B   A gas or telephone bill
   C   An application form or your curriculum vitae
   D   Proof of a bank account

349 **Who should you ask to be a referee for a job application? Select two options from below**
- A   A close personal friend
- B   A college tutor
- C   A previous employer
- D   A relative or family member

350 **When looking for employment, what is the purpose of a referee?**
- A   To write a report about a person's suitability for a job
- B   To search for jobs that match your skills
- C   To negotiate pay after a successful interview
- D   To resolve any disputes between you and your employer

351 **When might you need a CRB check?**
- A   When applying for welfare benefits
- B   When buying a house
- C   When requesting medical treatment from the NHS
- D   When applying for work that involves children or vulnerable people

352 **In Northern Ireland, it is legal to discriminate on grounds of religious belief or political opinion. Is this statement true or false?**
- A   True
- B   False

353 Most of the laws protecting people at work apply equally to people doing part-time or full-time jobs. Is this statement true or false?
   A   True
   B   False

354 By law, men and women who do the same job should receive equal pay. Is this statement true or false?
   A   True
   B   False

355 Select the correct statement
   A   It is illegal to discriminate against someone for the purposes of employment in any circumstances
   B   Discrimination is not against the law when the job involves working for someone in their own home

356 What types of discrimination can the Equal Opportunities Commission help with?
   A   Racial discrimination
   B   Discrimination related to disability
   C   Sex discrimination
   D   Religious discrimination

357 Select the correct statement
   A   It is illegal to pay workers below the minimum wage
   B   It is legal to pay workers below the minimum wage as long as they agree to the wage rate

358 It is legal for your employer to force you to work more hours than has been agreed in your contract. Is this statement true or false?

A True

B False

359 How many weeks of paid holiday each year are employees over 16 normally entitled to?

A Four weeks

B Five weeks

C Three weeks

D Two weeks

360 What information must an employer show on pay slips? Select two options from below

A National Insurance contributions that have been deducted from your pay

B Tax that has been deducted from your pay

C The date that your contract started

D The number of days' holiday entitlement that you have remaining

361 Select the correct statement from below

A If you are self-employed then you need to pay your own tax

B People who are self-employed have tax automatically taken from their earnings

362 Which of these statements is correct?

   A   The HM Revenue & Customs self-assessment helpline can provide help and advice on filling out tax forms

   B   You can only get help filling out tax forms by paying for the services of an accountant

363 What happens if you do not pay enough NI contributions? Select two options from below

   A   You may not receive a full State Pension

   B   You will be fined and need to sign up to a repayment plan

   C   You will be prosecuted and may face a prison sentence

   D   You will not be entitled to certain benefits such as Jobseeker's Allowance or Maternity Pay

364 What are National Insurance contributions used for? Select two options from below

   A   To contribute to your State Pension

   B   To help fund the National Health Service

   C   To pay for education and community services

   D   To pay for police and armed services

365 **What is the purpose of a National Insurance number?**

  A To prove that you have British nationality

  B To track National Insurance contributions

  C To allow companies to check your credit history

  D To prove that you have adequate home insurance

366 **At what age do young people receive their National Insurance number?**

  A 18 years old

  B 20 years old

  C 14 years old

  D 16 years old

367 **Select the correct statement**

  A Refugees who have had successful asylum applications can only work in specific areas

  B Refugees who have had successful asylum applications have the same rights to work as UK citizens

368 **Where can you apply for a National Insurance number? Select two options from below**

  A Any Jobcentre Plus branch

  B Your local council or town hall

  C Your local library

  D Your local social security office

369 **At what age can women get a State Pension?**
- A 60 years old
- B 65 years old
- C 55 years old
- D 70 years old

370 **At what age can men get a State Pension?**
- A 55 years old
- B 60 years old
- C 70 years old
- D 65 years old

371 **Select the correct statement**
- A Many people receive pensions through their work or pay into personal pension plans
- B People can only pay into and receive the State Pension

372 **Who should you speak to if you have health and safety concerns in your workplace? Select two answers from below**
- A The police
- B Your local MP
- C Your supervisor or manager
- D Your trade union representative

373 **Which of these statements is correct?**
- A Employees have no responsibility to work safely
- B Employers have a legal duty to make sure the workplace is safe

374 **You can be dismissed for raising health and safety concerns. Is this statement true or false?**

A True

B False

375 **What do trade unions aim to achieve for their members? Select two options from below**

A To provide advice and support on problems at work

B To deduct tax from their earnings

C To improve their pay and working conditions

D To limit overall pay increases

376 **Your employer can dismiss you for being a union member. Is this statement true or false?**

A True

B False

377 **It is compulsory for employees to join a trade union. Is this statement true or false?**

A True

B False

378 If an employee's work, punctuality or attendance does not improve, after being given a warning, then their employer can give them notice to leave their job. Is this statement true or false?

A True

B False

379 For what reason could you be immediately dismissed from your job?

A Because of your sexuality

B Because of your age

C Because of your religious beliefs

D Because of serious misconduct

380 When might you be entitled to redundancy pay? Select two options from below

A If you are dismissed from your job

B If you meet performance targets set by your employer

C The employer cannot afford to pay for the job

D The job is no longer needed by the employer

381 Between what ages can women claim the Jobseeker's Allowance?

A 21–65 years old

B 18–60 years old

C 18–65 years old

D 16–65 years old

382 **Select the correct statement**
- A You must be 16 or 17 years old to be eligible for a Young Person's Bridging Allowance
- B You must be at least 18 years old to be eligible for a Young Person's Bridging Allowance

383 **Between what ages can men claim the Jobseeker's Allowance?**
- A 21–65 years old
- B 18–60 years old
- C 16–65 years old
- D 18–65 years old

384 **Which of the following statements is correct?**
- A As soon as you become self-employed you should register yourself for National Insurance and tax by contacting HM Revenue & Customs
- B It is not necessary to contact HM Revenue & Customs when you become self-employed

385 **British citizens require a work permit before they can work in any country that is a member of the European Economic Area. Is this statement true or false?**
- A True
- B False

386 All women workers are entitled to Maternity Pay. Is this statement true or false?

A True
B False

387 Select the correct statement

A Maternity leave rights apply to both full-time and part-time workers
B Only women who have full-time employment are entitled to maternity leave

388 Women are only entitled to maternity leave after they have completed their first year in a job. Is this statement true or false?

A True
B False

389 Select the correct statement

A Men are always entitled to paternity leave
B Men must have worked for their employer at least 26 weeks before they are entitled to paternity leave

390 How many weeks of paid paternity leave are men entitled to?

A One week
B Two weeks
C Three weeks
D Four weeks

391 **The employment of children in the UK is strictly controlled by law. Is this statement true or false?**

A True

B False

392 **What do children aged 14 to 16 need from their local authority if they want to work? Select two options from below**

A A National Insurance number

B An employment card

C Certificate of fitness for work

D Proof of identity

393 **Select the correct statement from below**

A Children aged 14 to 16 can be employed to do any form of work as long as they are properly trained

B It is illegal to employ children aged 14 to 16 to do work that might cause them any kind of injury

394 **It is illegal for a child to work for more than one hour before school starts. Is this statement true or false?**

A True

B False

395 New Deal is a government programme that provides help and support to unemployed people to get back into work. Is this statement true or false?

A True
B False

396 What is the maximum number of hours that a child can work on a school day or Sunday?

A Eight hours
B Four hours
C Six hours
D Two hours

397 What is the maximum number of hours that a child may work before they must take a one-hour rest break?

A 10 hours
B 4 hours
C 6 hours
D 8 hours

398 Select the correct statement

A Children are free to work at any time of the day
B It is illegal for a child to work before 7am or after 7pm

399 **What is the maximum number of hours that a child can work in any school week?**

A   12 hours

B   18 hours

C   20 hours

D   38 hours

400 **Which of the following statements is correct?**

A   Children must apply for a National Insurance number when they get their first job

B   Children receive their National Insurance number just before their 16th birthday

ANSWERS

CHAPTER 1:
A CHANGING SOCIETY

1 **A** New laws were introduced restricting immigration to Britain

2 **B** To escape religious persecution

3 **B** 45%

4 **B** False

5 **A** In the 1960s and 1970s Parliament passed laws giving women the right to equal pay

6 **A** 1928

7 **C** 1918

8 **A** 1918

9 **A** Campaigners for greater rights for women

10 **D** 1882

11 **D** 1857

12 **B** In 19th-century Britain, women had fewer rights than men

13 **B** False

14 **D** United States, Australia, South Africa and New Zealand

15	**A**	True
16	**A**	Uganda
	C	South East Asia
17	**A**	To recruit workers to drive buses
18	**A**	To resolve a shortage of labour in the UK
19	**B**	Pakistan
	D	India
20	**D**	6 years
21	**C**	Ireland, other parts of Europe and the West Indies
22	**C**	1939–1945
23	**B**	To escape racist attacks
24	**D**	Poland, Ukraine, Belarus
25	**A**	To escape famine
26	**C**	16 years old
27	**B**	It is illegal to possess cannabis anywhere
28	**B**	It is illegal to be drunk in public
29	**C**	18 years old
30	**C**	Two million
31	**A**	Deliver newspapers
	C	Work in supermarkets or newsagents
32	**B**	A period of time taken by a young person to work or travel before starting university
33	**C**	One in three
34	**B**	True

35 **B** 16 years old

36 **A** One in five

37 **C** 17 and 18 years old

38 **D** 7 and 11

39 **A** 14

40 **A** It is compulsory for children aged between 5 and 16 to receive full-time education

41 **C** 65%

42 **B** 25%

43 **A** 10%

44 **B** Every week

45 **C** 15 million

46 **C** The average hourly pay rate is 20% lower for women

47 **B** True

48 **D** Three quarters

49 **A** Some young people work to pay for their university fees and expenses

CHAPTER 2:
UK TODAY – A PROFILE

50	**A**	False
51	**A**	23 April
52	**C**	Approximately 870 miles (1,400 kilometres)
53	**C**	Liverpool
54	**A**	London
55	**A**	Tyneside
56	**C**	Gaelic
57	**B**	29% of London's population
58	**B**	True
59	**B**	England
60	**C**	Approximately 3%
61	**A**	True
62	**C**	Around 10%
63	**B**	Seven people out of ten
64	**B**	75%
65	**C**	30 November
66	**B**	5.1 million
67	**B**	True
68	**C**	Because Britain was at war
69	**D**	1.7 million
70	**B**	About 50 million

71	**A**	2.9 million
72	**A**	About 60 million
73	**C**	84%
74	**B**	True
75	**D**	45%
76	**D**	Muslim
77	**D**	A count of the whole population
78	**C**	St Andrew
79	**D**	Once every ten years
80	**B**	2011
81	**A**	1801
82	**C**	100 years
83	**B**	About 8%
84	**A**	Give them sweets or chocolates
85	**C**	St George
86	**B**	1 January
87	**A**	14 February
88	**D**	Send anonymous cards to someone they secretly admire
89	**B**	People play jokes on each other
90	**A**	1 April
91	**D**	People give cards or gifts to their mothers
92	**D**	25 December
93	**A**	31 October

94	**B**	The birth of Jesus Christ
95	**C**	The evening of 5 November
96	**C**	The failure of a plot to bomb Parliament
97	**A**	Poppies
98	**C**	11 November
99	**D**	The memory of those who died fighting in wars
100	**C**	A horse race
101	**D**	The Sunday three weeks before Easter
102	**D**	Presbyterian
103	**D**	St Patrick
104	**C**	1 March
105	**D**	St David
106	**A**	17 March
107	**A**	True
108	**C**	The monarch makes the selection based on the choice of the Prime Minister and a committee appointed by the Church of England
109	**D**	The Anglican Church
110	**B**	Turkey
111	**A**	True
112	**B**	Tennis
113	**B**	In the 1530s
114	**D**	Anyone who is not Protestant

115 **A** St Patrick's Day in Northern Ireland

116 **A** Boxing Day and New Year are both public holidays

117 **A** 26 December

118 **B** Supreme Governor

CHAPTER 3:
HOW THE UNITED KINGDOM IS GOVERNED

119 **D** 1999

120 **C** About 20

121 **B** To make decisions about government policy

122 **C** Lord Chancellor

123 **A** The Opposition

124 **C** Senior members of the main opposition party

125 **B** To keep order during political debates
　　　C To make sure rules are followed in the House of Commons

126 **D** Elected by fellow MPs

127 **B** False

128 **A** True

129 **C** Political neutrality
　　　D Professionalism

130 **B** A manager or administrator who carries out government policy

131 **A** Defence
　　　C Foreign affairs

132 **C** England

133 **B** Chancellor of the Exchequer

134 **D** All of the above

135 **A** House of Commons

136 **C** Proportional representation

137 **B** Environment
D Transport

138 **B** Cardiff

139 **A** Edinburgh

140 **B** Education
D Health

141 **A** True

142 **D** 1922

143 **A** An unwritten constitution

144 **B** 1997

145 **A** Ensure attendance of MPs at voting time in the House of Commons
D Responsible for discipline in their party

146 **C** The King or Queen

147 **A** False

148 **C** The Prince of Wales

149 **B** Opening of a new parliamentary session

150 **C** At least every five years

151 **B** Prime Minister's Questions take place every week when Parliament is sitting

152 **A** The House of Commons is the more important of the two chambers in Parliament

153 **B** True

154 **C** "First past the post" system

155 **A** Win the most votes out of all candidates in their constituency

156 **C** Lord Chancellor

157 **B** False

158 **B** False

159 **A** Home Secretary

160 **A** Appoint the members of the Cabinet
C Leader of the party in power

161 **A** 10 Downing Street

162 **B** Represent their constituency
C Scrutinise and comment on what the government is doing

163 **A** True

164 **C** The party that wins the majority of constituencies forms the government

165 **C** Propose new laws
D Suggest amendments to laws

166 **D** By their party leaders

167 **A** True

168 **A** A member of the House of Lords who has been appointed by the Prime Minister

169 **D** 1958

170 **D** Every five years

171 **C** Large libraries
D Internet

172 **B** False

173 **D** Weekly

174 **D** Chequers

175   **B**   False

176   **B**   Subject to some restrictions, citizens of the European Union have the right to work in any EU member state

177   **A**   Write to your local MP
        B   Queue at the public entrance

178   **A**   18 years

179   **C**   Being a member of the armed forces
        D   Having been found guilty of a criminal offence

180   **A**   A connection with the area in which they wish to take office

181   **B**   False

182   **D**   53 member states

183   **C**   The Queen

184   **C**   1973

185   **D**   27 countries

186   **B**   Every year

187   **A**   For member states to function as a single market

188   **A**   Brussels

189   **A**   True

190   **A**   Administer EU funding programmes
        B   Draft proposals for new EU policies and laws

191   **C**   Examine decisions made by the European Council and the European Commission

192   **A**   True

193 **B** False

194 **C** To develop conventions which focus on human rights, democracy, education, the environment, health and culture

195 **B** False

196 **A** True

197 **D** 1949

198 **D** To prevent war and promote international peace and security

199 **A** Member of the UN Security Council

200 **B** False

201 **B** False

202 **A** Government taxation

203 **B** False

204 **A** True

205 **D** No, but they can ask Parliament to consider doing so

206 **B** A judge can only decide on the penalty for a person found guilty of a serious crime

207 **A** If a person is accused of having committed a minor crime

208 **D** To decide if someone is innocent or guilty of a serious crime

209 **D** The Metropolitan Police

210 **C** The Independent Police Complaints Commission

211   **B**   False

212   **A**   All reporting on radio and television must be balanced

      D   Television channels have to give equal time to rival viewpoints

213   **D**   Contact your local council election registration office

214   **B**   European elections

      C   Local elections

215   **A**   True

216   **A**   Both UK born and naturalised citizens have the right to vote

217   **B**   False

218   **A**   1969

219   **A**   The Metropolitan Police is based at New Scotland Yard

220   **B**   False

221   **B**   False

222   **B**   Proceedings in Parliament are publicly available

223   **B**   Hansard

224   **B**   A non-departmental public body

225   **B**   False

226   **D**   18 years old

CHAPTER 4:
EVERYDAY NEEDS

227 **A** Over the telephone

228 **A** If you lose your cash or debit card you must inform the bank immediately

229 **C** Proof of your address
D Proof of your identity

230 **B** False

231 **A** True

232 **A** £2

233 **B** If you are refused a loan you have the right to ask the reason why

234 **B** The local authority
D Your landlord

235 **D** 18 years old

236 **A** 25%

237 **B** False

238 **B** Council Tax
C Grants from central government

239 **A** True

240 **B** 2002

241 **A** If you need to see a specialist for medical treatment then you must see your GP first

242 **C** Two-thirds

243 **D** People who are unable to travel

244 **C** The local health authority

245 **C** As soon as you move to a new area

246 **C** You will be charged interest

247 **A** If you have a dispute with your neighbour then you may be able to avoid going to court by using a mediator

248 **B** 112
D 999

249 **B** Group practices of General Practitioners are sometimes called Primary Health Care Centres

250 **B** National Health Service

251 **B** People who do not have legal rights of residence in the UK

252 **B** False

253 **C** Citizens Advice Bureau
D Jobcentre Plus

254 **B** False

255 **B** In an emergency you should go to the Accident and Emergency department of your nearest hospital

256 **A** Everyone is entitled to apply for council accommodation

257 **D** Council housing

258 **B** A solicitor

259 **A** True

260 **A** The local authority

261 **C** A solicitor
D An estate agent

262 **B** When you rent a home privately you sign a tenancy agreement or lease

263 **A** So that you can withdraw if there are reasons you cannot complete the purchase

264 **B** False

265 **A** In your home
B At a clinic

266 **A** A bank
B A building society

267 **A** True

268 **D** A surveyor

269 **A** True

270 **B** False

271 **C** 240 volts

272 **A** True

273 **D** Water rates

274 **B** Citizens Advice Bureau
D The housing department of the local authority

275 **A** True

276 **A** True

277 **B** False

278 **C** To help you pay your rent

279 **B** After a tenancy agreement has been signed, a landlord cannot raise the rent without agreement from the tenant

280 **B** To cover the cost of any damage to the property

281 **A** True

282 **A** A list of all furniture and fittings in a property

283 **B** False

284 **A** To the local authority

285 **A** Preserve important buildings and countryside in the UK

286 **B** False

287 **A** True

288 **B** 11pm

289 **A** True

290 **A** True

291 **C** 18 years old

292 **A** 17 years old

293 **B** False

294 **C** Suitable for anyone aged four years or over

295 **A** No one younger than 18 may see an 18-rated film under any circumstances

296 **A** Suitable for everyone but some parts of the film might be unsuitable for children

297 **B** False

298 **C** ESOL

299 **A** True

300 **A** When applying for Housing Benefit
B When opening a bank account

301 **C** Give your details to the other driver
D Make a note of everything that happened and contact your insurance company

302 **B** False

303 **D** 60 miles per hour

304 **A** 70 miles per hour

305 **A** Tickets for trains are usually bought before you get on the train

306 **D** Every year

307 **B** False

308 **A** It is a criminal offence to have a car without motor insurance

309 **A** True

310 **A** True

311 **A** True

312 **B** Pass a practical driving test
C Pass a written theory test

313 **B** 30 miles per hour

314 **B** 11

315 **A** True

316 **C** 16

317 **B** False

318 **A** A 22-year-old university student

319 **B** Contraception

      D Sexual heath

320 **B** 12

321 **B** You can get regular antenatal care from your local hospital, local health centre or from special antenatal clinics

322 **A** True

323 **B** False

324 **B** Some dentists have two sets of charges, both NHS and private

325 **B** False

326 **B** An in-patient

327 **A** Six weeks

328 **C** 2,500

329 **A** A driving licence or a recent phone bill may be used to prove your identity

330 **B** Careers Wales

331 **A** True

332 **C** EAL teacher

333 **B** 7, 11 and 14

334 **A** Parents are allowed to withdraw their children from religious education lessons

335 **A** True

336 **B** False

337 **B** 11

338 **B** Integrated schools

339 **A** True

340 **B** False

341 **C** The local education authority

342 **B** 11

343 **A** 190 days

344 **A** About 8%

CHAPTER 5:
EMPLOYMENT

345   **B**   False

346   **B**   Employers have to check that everyone they employ is legally entitled to work in the UK

347   **B**   By contacting the National Academic Recognition Information Centre

348   **A**   A covering letter or letter of application
        C   An application form or your curriculum vitae

349   **B**   A college tutor
        C   A previous employer

350   **A**   To write a report about a person's suitability for a job

351   **D**   When applying for work that involves children or vulnerable people

352   **B**   False

353   **A**   True

354   **A**   True

355   **B**   Discrimination is not against the law when the job involves working for someone in their own home

356   **C**   Sex discrimination

357   **A**   It is illegal to pay workers below the minimum wage

358   **B**   False

359   **A**   Four weeks

360 **A** National Insurance contributions that have been deducted from your pay
B Tax that has been deducted from your pay

361 **A** If you are self-employed then you need to pay your own tax

362 **A** The HM Revenue & Customs self-assessment helpline can provide help and advice on filling out tax forms

363 **A** You may not receive a full State Pension
D You will not be entitled to certain benefits such as Jobseeker's Allowance or Maternity Pay

364 **A** To contribute to your State Pension
B To help fund the National Health Service

365 **B** To track National Insurance contributions

366 **D** 16 years old

367 **B** Refugees who have had successful asylum applications have the same rights to work as UK citizens

368 **A** Any Jobcentre Plus branch
D Your local social security office

369 **A** 60 years old

370 **D** 65 years old

371 **A** Many people receive pensions through their work or pay into personal pension plans

372 **C** Your supervisor or manager
D Your trade union representative

373 **B** Employers have a legal duty to make sure the workplace is safe

374 **B** False

375 **A** To provide advice and support on problems at work
C To improve their pay and working conditions

376 **B** False

377 **B** False

378 **A** True

379 **D** Because of serious misconduct

380 **C** The employer cannot afford to pay for the job
D The job is no longer needed by the employer

381 **B** 18–60 years old

382 **A** You must be 16 or 17 years old to be eligible for a Young Person's Bridging Allowance

383 **D** 18–65 years old

384 **A** As soon as you become self-employed you should register yourself for National Insurance and tax by contacting HM Revenue & Customs

385 **B** False

386 **B** False

387 **A** Maternity leave rights apply to both full-time and part-time workers

388 **B** False

389 **B** Men must have worked for their employer at least 26 weeks before they are entitled to paternity leave

390 **B** Two weeks

391 **A** True

392 **B** An employment card
C Certificate of fitness for work

393 **B** It is illegal to employ children aged 14 to 16
to do work that might cause them any kind of
injury

394 **A** True

395 **A** True

396 **D** Two hours

397 **B** 4 hours

398 **B** It is illegal for a child to work before 7am or
after 7pm

399 **A** 12 hours

400 **B** Children receive their National Insurance
number just before their 16th birthday

NOTES

NOTES